NLP

Comprehensive Handbook For Adeptly Utilizing Manipulation Techniques And Harnessing The Power Of Persuasion

(Acquire Knowledge On NLP And Its Potential Benefits In Enhancing Personal And Business Success)

Clyde Bruce

TABLE OF CONTENT

What Is The Power Of Use Of NLP ? 1

The Selection Process Of Toxic Individuals In Targeting Their Preferred Victims 27

Narcissism 58

Simple Agoraphobia NLP Exercises 76

Develop Exceptional Communication Skills Through Neuro-Linguistic Programming (NLP) 82

How NLP Works 106

What Is The Scheduled Commencement Time Of The Presentation? 137

What Is The Power Of Use Of NLP ?

There exist numerous rationales for pursuing the study of NLP , chiefly centered around gaining insights into the intricacies of human behavior and understanding one's cognitive self-perception. Our objective is to utilize these skill sets effectively in practical settings, where they can create a substantial impact.

NLP is of utmost importance in the contemporary era. We exist in a contemporary society characterized by relentless technological progress, continuously fostering connections with colleagues, loved ones, and individuals of significance. We are constantly engaged in responding to inquiries, leaving little room for introspection.

In the subsequent sections, you will uncover cognitive patterns and acquire techniques to effectively regulate them, both in your personal capacity and while overseeing others.

You will acquire a novel approach towards interpersonal interactions and gain insight into the thoughts and emotions of others.

Gaining insight into the functioning of our cognitive faculties.

We possess an identical neural circuitry in our central nervous system, acquire a multitude of shared knowledge and learning experiences, and perhaps share concerns about comparable subjects. Nevertheless, it is important to acknowledge that our cognitive processes are not universally uniform. Each individual possesses their own unique perspective, with thoughts and opinions that vary significantly, akin to the distinctiveness of our fingerprints.

Unbeknownst to us, we gradually acclimate to minor irritations and encounter emotional and cognitive boundaries throughout our existence. It is imperative for individuals to define and safeguard boundaries in order to cultivate a sense of personal security and elicit others' adherence to our decisions.

Behaviors such as the ability to engage in public speaking, modifying detrimental habits into beneficial ones, assuming greater responsibility in various aspects, all offer the potential to exceed our current capacities. Nonetheless, it is disheartening that numerous individuals abandon their attempts soon after, citing the notion that "an old parrot cannot learn to speak." However, such claims hold no factual basis.

It necessitates the utilization of appropriate tools to accomplish the task. Through the identification of cognitive patterns, one can delve further to implement the necessary modifications. The most effective approach towards accomplishing transformative outcomes lies in comprehending the underlying mechanisms for emotional production and actively striving to alter them.

How can one cultivate or generate emotions within oneself?

They experience inherent stimuli upon birth, such as the sensation of the coffee maker in operation and the aroma of coffee upon waking, the sound of a crying child or barking dog requiring attention, recent news updates on their favored website, or the presence of a television emitting sound. All of these occurrences are neural stimulations taking place within your cerebral function.

Once this information is received, it is promptly analyzed, and assigned a significance that embodies an emotional essence. You gave this feeling. One may perceive it as a positive occurrence - the joyful dog, the melodic sound of the coffee maker, the momentarily distressed child who will soon be comforted with affection. A day of great potential lies ahead. Conversely, one might experience feelings of frustration due to the persistent barking of the dog and the ceaseless crying of the child. Tears cascade as the coffee maker remains void of its dark elixir.

Both of the aforementioned scenarios serve as stimuli, evoking distinct meaning and emotion that consequently elicits a specific response. Through the comprehension of emotions and the significance attributed to thoughts, one has the ability to revisit those thoughts and endeavor to effectuate their transformation. To illustrate, it is possible to record one's thoughts and subsequently select more effective responses.

The matter at hand pertains to the frequent occurrence in which our awareness is limited to the initial stimulus, while the comprehension of the emotion associated with that stimulus lies beyond the confines of our consciousness. Attempt to articulate ideas in the following manner:

I experience a sense of contentment in your presence.

\\\"You made me angry\\\".

The actions of that client have significantly disrupted the course of my day.

Irrespective of the manner in which these expressions are constructed, it is important to note that the true source of my emotional state does not stem from the actions or words of the other individual. It is we who consistently ascribe significance to all the circumstances we encounter. The emotional state experienced by individuals is not derived from external factors, including either other individuals or the environment. Hence, it can be concluded that no causal relationship can be established. The evidence for this assertion lies in the fact that diverse emotional states arise from identical circumstances among distinct individuals.

In this regard, it is infeasible for anyone to induce a particular emotion within us. The occurrence entails an individual engaging in an action, followed by my internal deliberation that leads to the association of an emotion with said action. Ultimately, the responsibility for our emotional state lies upon us, irrespective of external circumstances.

Identify Limiting Belief

It has become evident that cultivating empowering beliefs and shedding limiting beliefs is of utmost significance in attaining success. The question is, \\\"How?\\\"

Prior to proceeding with the task, it is imperative for you to ascertain whether we possess any obstructive beliefs that may impede our progress. Hello, if you do not possess a limiting belief, what is it that you ought to eradicate? My acquaintance displayed a strong desire to unearth various forms of constraining convictions, and even proceeded to voice dissatisfaction, questioning, 'Why am I unable to identify my cognitive obstacle?' The absence of its discovery implies its nonexistence, thereby rendering the notion of locating it implausible. The discovery has revealed that the absence of concern can indeed transform into a novel cognitive obstacle.

Upon establishing a goal, it is important to evaluate one's emotions and physical sensations. Is there any discomforts? Alternatively, do you experience any sensations of tension or discomfort in any particular areas of your body?

If the answer is negative, then you are safe. There is no aspect of yourself that opposes the objective.

However, if such circumstances do exist, they indicate a manifestation of the inhibiting belief that opposes the pursuit of the objective.

You might also encounter individuals who have successfully attained the objective you aspire to accomplish. To acquire wealth, observe individuals who possess abundant riches. What is your perception upon observing them? If one were to hold the belief that, 'This world is unjust.' They achieve wealth through the unauthorized acquisition of others' assets. If one harbors such a pessimistic perspective, it indicates the presence of a constraining conviction concerning financial matters.

If your intention is to achieve weight loss, and when you encounter individuals who possess a slender physique, you may often find yourself remarking, 'That individual appears exceptionally slim.' I earnestly aspire to possess a physique akin to that, yet regrettably, attaining such a body is unfeasible for me. This predicament is indicative of a constraining conviction.

If one entertains the notion, 'I am confident in my ability to achieve wealth, akin to those individuals,' or 'I am committed to following my dietary regimen in order to attain a slender physique, similar to hers,' this can be regarded as an indication of a transformative conviction. There is no requirement for any action to be taken regarding your belief. Exert maximum effort and you will likewise attain comparable levels of success.

An alternate approach entails practicing sincerity and evaluating your achievements. Have you ever encountered a situation where despite your efforts, you were unable to attain a goal or objective? You are cognizant of the attainability of the objective and your ability to conquer it, yet inexplicably, you are unable to actualize it. Indeed, that is indicative of a constraining belief that is impeding, obstructing, and unsettling your progress.

Once you have become aware of the presence of a constraining belief, it is imperative to ascertain the specific nature of this belief in order to proceed with its eradication. Individuals who possess previous experience or familiarity with the technique of self-hypnosis will discover this exercise effortless to engage in, whereas those who have yet to engage in self-hypnosis are encouraged to attempt it by adhering to the straightforward instructions provided.

1. Seek out a tranquil setting wherein you can unwind, allocate a minimum of 15 minutes or ideally 30 minutes, and ensure complete absence of disturbances such as television, phone, or any extraneous audio. If you so desire, you may also opt to secure the room.

2. Please ready a writing utensil and a sheet of paper. Please find a comfortable seating position and allow yourself to relax. Feel free to indulge in the soothing melodies of the relaxation music, should you desire. Subsequently, record the objectives you aspire to accomplish.

3. When formulating your objectives, if you encounter signs of rejection or hear whispers of failure, they indicate the presence of a constraining belief. When formulating your objective, the presence of a constraining belief may serve as a reminder of previous setbacks or prevailing societal perspectives regarding your aspirations. Uncertainty and apprehension will rapidly envelop your hearts.

4. Please enumerate each obstacle, rejection, or negative emotion that you experience by documenting them

chronologically. Do not engage in physical confrontation, verbal disagreement, or opposition. Instead, adopt a state of calm and receptiveness while accommodating the expressions of protest and criticism. If one were to resist, generally they would be rendered speechless. However, they will manipulate your subconscious mind to undermine all of your endeavors.

5. Have you completed the task? Certainly, the statements you have written can be classified as your self-imposed limitations. Please retain possession of this list. Our objective is to eliminate its contents by altering the submodalities, however, it is essential that we first acquire knowledge on the subject of submodality.

Psychopathy

Curiously, there exists a minimal proportion of personnel within the professional environment. Nevertheless, these individuals must not be trivialized as their capacity to inflict permanent harm upon a company or organization, particularly when occupying senior management roles, should not be overlooked. Surprisingly, this phenomenon is frequently observed among the upper echelons of organizations, affording them the capacity and authority to propagate their alarming behavior, thereby causing repercussions that permeate the entire establishment. Consequently, their behaviors tend to exert considerable influence on the organizational culture of a company, and undoubtedly, an unsatisfactory culture is one that fails to prioritize the emotional well-being of its employees. The impacts stemming from the conduct of individuals with psychopathic traits within the organizational context.

Individuals exhibiting psychopathic tendencies in professional environments adapt their behaviors based on their circumstances. For instance, it is possible for them to exhibit charisma and amiability towards individuals of higher authority in a hierarchical structure while simultaneously manifesting abusive behaviors towards subordinates occupying lower positions within the organizational hierarchy. Thus, they exhibit diverse manifestations of their identity to various personnel. There exist certain nuanced distinctions among individuals exhibiting psychopathic traits. As an illustration, it is worth noting the existence of high-achieving individuals with psychopathic traits, specifically those who become associated with white-collar criminal activities. It is likely that they originate from advantaged socio-economic backgrounds and possess a minimal susceptibility to consequences, combined with a high level of intelligence, thus forming a foundation for achieving success in the manifestation of psychopathic tendencies. On the opposing side, we encounter the inefficacious psychopath who becomes entangled in conventional criminal activities, possesses a diminished level of cognitive abilities, resulting in an elevated likelihood of severe legal consequences.

"Allow me to present an intriguing piece of information for your consideration:

According to clinical criteria, a percentage of up to 1 from the overall population can be categorized as psychopathic. Moreover, it is observed that the realm of business often harbors a higher prevalence of individuals with psychopathic traits compared to the overall populace, particularly within the ranks of senior leadership. The dark triad is anticipated to encompass other professional groups, such as attorneys, individuals in the media sector, journalists, police personnel, chefs, religious leaders, and physicians.

Furthermore, we shall now delve into the subject matter of the Organizational Psychopath.

Typically, these individuals possess an inherent desire to attain a godlike status, exerting dominance over others and gravitating towards senior positions within the organizational hierarchy. This particular work arrangement is favored by them due to its capacity to enable the exercise of control over as many individuals as feasible, as elucidated earlier. Political figures, chief executive officers, and individuals in managerial positions frequently belong to this classification.

They display qualities of intellect, charm, wit, occasional sincerity, and captivate in their communication. They possess remarkable speed and proficiency in swiftly discerning an individual's desires, allowing them to expeditiously craft a narrative that aligns with the person's expectations. Typically, they employ manipulation tactics to compel individuals into complying with their desires, which encompasses not only their professional tasks but also taking credit for the efforts exerted by others, all the while offloading their own responsibilities onto subordinate team members. They exhibit a limited threshold for interacting with individuals and demonstrate superficial expressions of emotions. They demonstrate an equal level of unpredictability, thereby rendering them unreliable in fulfilling their contractual obligations. Moreover, they cannot be relied upon to assume complete accountability in the event of any mishap.

Therefore, in situations where organizations are plagued with abusive supervision, psychopaths are positioned to gain a competitive edge and flourish. This is attributed to their heightened ability to withstand stress and endure interpersonal mistreatment, thereby disregarding the importance of cultivating positive relationships with their colleagues.

Psychopathic individuals ascend the corporate hierarchy and acquire the know-how to sustain their authority through a series of steps, as delineated hereafter:

Introduction: Owing to their exceedingly refined social abilities, individuals with psychopathic traits possess a distinct advantage in securing employment within various organizational settings. Given their enchanting charisma and astute mental acuity, discerning the presence of psychopathic tendencies within them may prove arduous for any observer at this juncture. Indeed, should you possess one within your professional setting, it is likely that you would recollect perceiving them as benevolent or advantageous.

Evaluation: In the process of evaluation, the average individual with psychopathic tendencies will gauge your potential value to them, measuring your utility on a scale. At this juncture, you can be classified as either a benefactor or a mere instrument in the situation. Pawns are maneuvered for the sake of personal advancement, while patrons assume a god-like status, necessitating satisfaction due to their formal authority and dependency on safeguarding within the game.

Manipulation: During this phase, the psychopath fabricates a psychopathic narrative wherein they manipulate perceptions concerning both themselves and others. Consequently, individuals will be presented with misleading information about others, leading them to project a favorable image of themselves. They manipulate your role as a pawn within his network, subtly compelling you to adopt their agenda without your conscious awareness.

Encounter: In this phase, it is common for the psychopath to impugn your character and that of others, in order to perpetuate the agenda that they compelled you to embrace at the outset. This is how one finds oneself assuming the position of either a subordinate or a benefactor.

Promotion: As individuals ascend in their professional growth, it becomes necessary for them to eliminate a valued patron in order to assume a role of authority and distinction. Please observe that this occurs to the detriment of a previously supportive individual.

Upon close examination of patterns, it becomes apparent that organizations are frequently inclined to recruit individuals exhibiting psychopathic traits. This phenomenon is detrimental. However, the following is the rationale behind this occurrence:

The majority of job descriptions have a tendency to appeal to individuals with psychopathic traits, as they imply that organizations possess an inherent inclination to engage with individuals who are willing to pursue success by any means necessary, even if it comes at the detriment of others. In certain instances, advertisements directly target this demographic. Furthermore, they are being actively sought out by organizations due to their charisma and knack for making favorable first impressions. Their appeal to employers lies in their propensity to appear emotionally stable, rational, and amicable, all of which are additional attributes sought after by the selection committee.

Moreover, their lack of accountability manifests in a manner that could potentially be misinterpreted as a propensity for calculated risk and entrepreneurialism, even by discerning interviewers. Their proclivity for seeking excitement, conversely,

It is possible that their attitude could be interpreted as eagerness for the job, and on certain occasions, even managers might actively support their endeavors. Their allure is often mistaken for an inherent magnetism, which inevitably leads to deleterious consequences in the long run. In conclusion, it is probable that they would falsify their educational accomplishments, including accolades, qualifications, and certifications, in order to create the impression of enhanced expertise.

Psychopaths may be selectively chosen for advancement due to their ability to exude charisma, composure, and decisiveness. Furthermore, they receive support through the utilization of their manipulative and coercive tactics. They employ their influence in order to implement a strategy of dividing and exercising control, subsequently ascending the corporate hierarchy and advancing their personal interests.

The Selection Process Of Toxic Individuals In Targeting Their Preferred Victims

Specific attributes and patterns of behavior render individuals more susceptible to manipulation, a fact that those possessing traits associated with dark psychology are acutely aware of. They have a propensity to target individuals with such particular behavioral attributes due to their inherent vulnerability. Allow us to delve into the characteristics exhibited by the preferred targets of manipulative individuals.

Psychological Vulnerability and Fragility

Manipulative individuals tend to exploit individuals who possess a vulnerability in their emotional well-being or are emotionally delicate. Regrettably, these victims encounter the predicament of having identifiable characteristics that can be easily discerned, even by individuals unknown to them in entirety. Consequently, adept manipulators find it simple to locate such individuals.

Individuals with a pronounced lack of emotional security often exhibit a heightened defensiveness in the face of criticism or stress, rendering their presence readily discernible within social contexts. Despite only a few interactions, a skilled manipulator can assess with a certain level of precision the extent of a person's insecurities. They shall endeavor to instigate their prospective targets through subtle means, subsequently observing their response. In the event that individuals exhibit an excessive defensive stance, manipulative individuals will interpret this as an indication of vulnerability and escalate their manipulative tactics.

In addition, manipulators possess the ability to discern if a target harbors emotional insecurities, as evidenced by their inclination to divert accusations or negative remarks. They will devise a means to place you in an uncomfortable position, and should you attempt to deflect or rationalize rather than directly addressing the matter, the manipulator may deduce that you possess insecurity and consequently deem you as susceptible to manipulation.

Individuals with social anxiety commonly exhibit emotional insecurity, a fact that manipulators are well cognizant of. In the context of social gatherings, they possess a keen ability to readily identify and subsequently exploit those who experience social anxiety. Practitioners of social dynamics possess the ability to discern females who exhibit signs of discomfort in social contexts through their observable behaviors. Social anxiety proves challenging to hide, particularly from manipulative individuals well-versed in exploiting emotional susceptibility.

The concept of emotional fragility diverges from that of emotional insecurity. Individuals who exhibit emotional insecurity frequently display it overtly, whereas emotionally fragile individuals may present as typical but are prone to emotional instability when faced with even minor triggers. Manipulators tend to hone in on individuals who exhibit emotional vulnerability, as these individuals are highly susceptible to eliciting a response. Upon discovering your susceptibility to emotional vulnerability, a manipulator will eagerly seize the opportunity to exploit you, well aware of the comparative ease with which this can be accomplished.

Temporary emotional vulnerability makes individuals with these characteristics susceptible to exploitation by manipulative opportunists. An individual could display emotional stability in the majority of instances, yet exhibit emotional vulnerability during a breakup, mourning, or when confronted with emotionally taxing circumstances. The increasingly malevolent schemers are capable of gaining your confidence, exercising patience, and anticipating your vulnerability. As an alternative, they can resort to unscrupulous tactics in order to precipitate emotional vulnerability in an individual they are focusing on.

Sensitive People

Individuals who possess a heightened sensitivity are characterized by their ability to process information at a profound level and exhibit a greater awareness of the intricacies present within social dynamics. They possess numerous commendable qualities as they consistently exhibit considerate behavior towards others and conscientiously take measures to prevent inflicting harm upon individuals, whether in a direct or indirect manner. Individuals of this nature generally exhibit a strong aversion towards acts of violence or cruelty. They possess a heightened sensitivity towards distressing news narratives or graphic portrayals of violence within cinematic productions, often becoming easily disturbed by such content.

Individuals who possess a heightened sensitivity are prone to experiencing emotional fatigue as a result of absorbing the emotions of others. Upon entering a room, they possess an innate capacity to perceive the emotional states of individuals around them, due to their inherent talent for discerning and comprehending nonverbal signals such as body language, facial expressions, and nuances in tone.

Maneuverers tend to set their sights on individuals who possess a heightened sensitivity, as they are particularly susceptible to manipulation. If you possess susceptibility to specific triggers, manipulators can exploit them to their advantage. They will simulate particular emotions with the intention of alluring vulnerable individuals in order to manipulate them.

Individuals who possess a high level of sensitivity also have a tendency to become easily frightened. They exhibit an elevated 'startle response', thereby displaying pronounced indications of fear or anxiety in circumstances that may be perceived as menacing. For instance, individuals with heightened sensitivity tend to exhibit a tendency to react impulsively when approached unexpectedly, without first assessing the presence of any legitimate threat. For individuals of a more sensitive disposition, concealing this aspect of their character can prove to be quite challenging, as individuals with ill intentions possess an innate ability to discern it effortlessly even from considerable distances.

Individuals with a proclivity for sensitivity often exhibit a proclivity for withdrawal as well. The majority of individuals in question exhibit introverted tendencies and possess a preference for solitude, as interpersonal interactions tend to deplete their emotional energy. Individuals with manipulative intentions often exhibit a tendency to focus on introverted individuals as their preferred targets, given that introversion can facilitate the isolation of potential victims.

Manipulators can additionally discern individuals who are sensitive by attentively observing their manner of communication. Individuals who possess a heightened sense of sensitivity are often characterized by their adherence to propriety, abstaining from the use of coarse or offensive language, and displaying a consistent commitment to politically correct discourse to ensure the prevention of any potential offense. Additionally, they demonstrate a propensity for politeness, frequently employing expressions of courtesy such as "please" and "thank you" in greater measure than their counterparts. Manipulators target such individuals due to their inherent politeness, as they recognize that these individuals are unlikely to immediately dismiss them. Sensitive individuals tend to accommodate others as they are averse to being impolite, which inadvertently provides an opportunity for malicious individuals to insert themselves into their lives.

Volume VI - Exemplifying Fourteen Instances of Utilizing Natural Language Processing

The following are fourteen prevalent instances where NLP has been frequently utilized to generate beneficial impacts in various aspects of life. Employ this compilation of ideas as a foundation for embarking upon an exploration of the various facets where NLP can be of assistance in enhancing the quality of your daily existence. The individual you have the potential to evolve into surpasses what you may presently discern.

Managing Grief

Mourning can serve as a potent point of reference linked to a particular stimulus, and comprehending the process of reconditioning that reference or surmounting it with a fresh perspective can bring about transformative effects. The purpose of existence lies in deriving pleasure from life, and acquiring knowledge on how to alleviate sorrow constitutes a significant advantage afforded by NLP . Grief arises from highly impactful, deeply emotional experiences, and unraveling these catalysts can present a monumental undertaking. Nevertheless, by demonstrating patience and unwavering determination, the task can be accomplished.

Alleviating and Eradicating Anxiety

Anxiety commonly arises from inadequate preparedness, leading to the anticipation that the current undertaking is destined to culminate in a state of failure or embarrassment. Participating in endeavors such as future pacing actively addresses this fundamental origin of anxiety, surpassing mere verbal affirmations of preparedness and instead allowing for the experience of readiness in advance.

Conquering fears and phobias

Fears can be regarded as an adverse influence, a conditioned response to a particular stimulus. Consequently, anxieties can be trained and surmounted. NLP techniques, including the swish method, provide us with a potent means to substitute feelings of anxiety and panic with emotions of tranquility and fortitude.

Dissociating Bad Memories

Negative or unpleasant memories tend to establish firm imprints within our minds, and can be accompanied by influential triggers. The recollection of a distressing event may be accompanied by a specific odor or physical feeling, and each instance of encountering this sensation elicits a cascade of adverse emotions. Navigating through life in this manner can have a debilitating impact. Natural Language Processing (NLP) holds promise as a viable approach for addressing this issue through the elimination or reconditioning of the responses evoked by these anchors, and potentially even by completely recontextualizing the negative memories. Research has demonstrated that the majority of individuals possess the tendency to rationalize and reframe adversities, thereby uncovering the underlying positives within those unfavorable experiences. The most transformative experiences for individuals often encompass the moments they consider as their bleakest. Devote ample time to comprehending the factors that elicit unfavorable recollections, and subsequently delve into the process of substituting those associations. Allocate sufficient time for inquiring thoughtfully, with the intention of reframing negative memories in a manner that allows you to perceive them as formative experiences that have contributed to shaping your present self.

Tackling Audacious Goals

Attainment of significant objectives necessitates thorough preparation and a resolute determination to triumph. The majority of the NLP techniques delineated herein can be utilized for a multitude of objectives. For instance, the practice of future pacing plays a paramount role in equipping oneself for the proceedings encompassing various endeavors, be it an arduous project or a decade-long strategy. Effectively controlling your habits and anchors is of utmost importance as it enables you to attain the necessary composure, patience, and mental clarity to effectively tackle demanding tasks. Gaining insight into the art of establishing enhanced rapport by employing mirroring techniques and demonstrating heightened attentiveness to submodalities can foster the necessary connections vital for achieving your ultimate objective.

TOPIC OF PERCEPTION: Assume an individual has a preference for pizza. They are fond of the flavor and aroma. The enjoyment derived from consuming pizza is solely attributed to the individual. The subjective perception pertains to our individual and intimately personal perspective of the world. It is exceedingly difficult to employ language in an attempt to articulate the experiences derived from visual perception, auditory perception, and gustatory perception – colloquially referred to as our senses. We possess inadequate aptitude in effectively articulating sensory experiences, such as the taste or scent of something. Despite positive endorsement of the pizza's flavor from a companion who is savoring it alongside you, we can never ascertain with certainty that we are experiencing identical gustatory perceptions. We employ linguistic expressions to convey a sensory experience, yet by attaching those expressions to disparate experiences.

An additional illustration pertains to the skies. Upon gazing upwards, we articulate that the celestial canopy is a shade of azure primarily due to the indoctrination received during our formative years. Nonetheless, the perception of observing the sky in its bluish hue is entirely subjective. The perception of the color "blue" may vary across individuals, and it is challenging to discern or express the subjective experience of perceiving the sky as blue for each person.

The realm of subjective experience encompasses various sensory perceptions, including emotions, enjoyment, sorrow, flavors, and scents, each unique to the individual. It constitutes a personal reality, unique to oneself and limited to each individual. You may elucidate upon the sensory experience of the pizza to someone, yet it remains impossible for them to comprehensively grasp or genuinely appreciate the depth of your perception. We can endeavor to attentively listen, exercise empathy, exhibit compassion, endure alongside, and strive to adopt the perspective of an individual with anorexia, yet we are ultimately unable to completely comprehend their subjective experience.

Consider it from Nathaniel's fresh perspective. A more formal way to express the same idea could be: "The objective methodology in creating a still-life depiction of a fruit bowl entails observing the fruit as spherical, possessing three-dimensional qualities, and either firm or delicate. These fruits are the consumable portions of plants that have evolved from flowers, displaying extension tissues." Not so yummy. The subjective perspective, acquired through the application of NLP techniques, would delineate that identical arrangement of fruit as enticing and piquant, fragrant and saccharine, tender to the tactile sense akin to that of an infant's skin, or furrowed resembling the brow of a bulldog. See the difference? Among the available options, envision the preference for painting or partaking in the consumption of a particular bowl of fruit.

Framing Negative Emotions

In my perspective, I hold the belief that a fundamental aspect of initiating the process of framing entails the elimination or reduction of adverse connotations associated with certain events. This is, in my estimation, the factor that significantly hinders individuals' progress, as I can personally attest. Begin by considering a past episode wherein you experienced an unfavorable outcome, causing you to hold a pessimistic perspective on the matter, much like the practice of dismantling an adverse association. This could entail not succeeding in your driving examination or encountering a subpar outcome in a job interview.

What you have accomplished is extracting one of these adverse memories from your hippocampus situated within the limbic system, subsequently projecting it as a visual representation or concise motion sequence within your prefrontal cortex, the cognitive region of the brain responsible for logical processing and comprehension. Furthermore, the amygdala will be solicited for emotional information and will, in all likelihood, furnish negative emotions such as fear, anxiety, or disappointment. The amygdala lacks temporal perception, resulting in emotions that retain their intensity, as if the event were unfolding anew in the present moment.

Allow us to consider the instance of an unsuccessful driving examination. I can personally identify with this one due to my lack of success in my initial endeavor. You might have diligently prepared and executed all maneuvers flawlessly under the guidance of your instructor in the weeks preceding the examination. Nevertheless, on the scheduled examination day, you arrived tardily at the driving center owing to inclement weather conditions and congested traffic, which consequently caused you to become flustered and rushed. Definitely not in a composed and tranquil disposition, prepared to embark on the journey personally.

Please envision the occurrence in question and endeavor to create a singular, lucid depiction that effectively captures and encapsulates the essence of that particular moment. It is possible that you are experiencing difficulties with stalling the vehicle during a hill start or spending time in the parking lot afterwards while feeling discouraged. Regardless of the nature of the subject, endeavor to establish a visual representation.

Now endeavor to adopt a detached standpoint from the situation, wherein you perceive the picture from a third-party outlook, observing it as if from an elevated position at the corner of the frame. Should you have already distanced yourself from the image, please proceed to withdraw even more and observe it from a heightened state of detachment, perhaps at a distance further down the street.

At present, you should possess the ability to perceive yourself distinctly within this image, a composition that impeccably encapsulates the instance of your unsuccessful completion of the driving assessment on that particular day. Nevertheless, your current objective entails deliberately adding a degree of blurriness to the image, while also incorporating a grainy texture and applying a black and white effect reminiscent of an antiquated film negative, as previously elucidated. In addition, enclose it within a physical frame resembling the vintage stainless steel frames often observed in cinematic portrayals of stately mansions. The image can now be observed to possess an altered texture, potentially resembling the delicate appearance of pastel paint.

The subsequent step involves displaying this picture on the wall, preferably in an art gallery or expansive residence, a location where individuals would casually observe it before proceeding with their activities with minimal attention or genuine curiosity.

Consequently, carefully contemplate that recollection or picture once again within the depths of your cognition. I introduced the illustration of an unsuccessful driving examination as it is a relatable experience for many individuals (however, you may substitute it with any comparable personal scenario). You will likely observe a significant reduction in the negative emotional content of the memory. It may still elicit a slight sense of discomfort, albeit significantly less than it previously did. The key is to revisit the aforementioned scenario, reproducing it alongside the associated imagery, including any other images that may be intertwined with the memory.

Arrange them all on the wall in close proximity and observe how their ability to elicit emotional responses has diminished. They have now transformed into mere fragments of the past, adorning the wall.

Physical communication

While it might not appear to be an urgent matter, the manner in which we engage in physical contact with others significantly contributes to our ability to exert influence over them, as suggested by scholars and practitioners of Neuro-Linguistic Programming (NLP). This phenomenon can be attributed to the innate inclination of human beings to seek physical contact. It is deeply ingrained within us to express our emotions and affection through acts such as embracing those dear to us, engaging in hand-holding gestures as a symbol of connection, and offering solace by holding our loved ones close during trying circumstances or moments of distress. Nevertheless, our inclination towards the tactile experience manifests at a relatively earlier stage. Indeed, we could contend that it is inherent to us from birth. Namely, infants—naive and unaffected—desire and indeed require the opportunity to encounter the tactile stimuli that arise from the act of being touched. Research consistently suggests that the sensations newborns derive from dozing off on their mother's bosom, near her pulsating heart, contribute significantly to their well-being and development.

Applying NLP techniques:

Despite its simplicity, a physical contact such as a handshake during an introduction or a friendly pat on the shoulder can foster a connection. A gentle physical gesture can indicate attentive listening and genuine concern for someone's words, as well as convey a sense of ease and the desire for mutual comfort in the presence of another person. Your tactile contact elicits a sense of personal connection, empathy, or comprehension, all of which are fundamental emotional needs that we, as individuals, seek during our interpersonal engagements. Presented here are several straightforward yet remarkably efficient NLP techniques involving physical touch, which can contribute to enhancing the comfort, relaxation, and connectedness experienced by individuals, thus fostering an increased receptiveness towards your suggestions.

Engage in a handshake—grasp someone's hand firmly and maintain the contact for a brief but perceptible duration. This will showcase your sincere enthusiasm and delight in making acquaintance with an individual. When individuals perceive your sincere interest in their words, they are inclined to divulge supplementary information.

Offer a gesture of acknowledgment by lightly tapping their shoulder, indicating that you have attentively listened and genuinely appreciated the content of their communication. Frequently, it signifies the establishment of a bond between two individuals or a high regard for someone. When establishing a connection or manifesting reverence, individuals are significantly more inclined to lend an ear and contemplate our individual viewpoints, in contrast to those who do not hold us in esteem or sense an attachment. This technique can also be implemented subsequent to expressing your viewpoint, with the intention of garnering concurrence and acceptance from others. Consider, for instance, a scenario wherein you have recently presented a business proposition to your supervisor and chief executive officer. As you exit the premises to grant them the opportunity to deliberate, briefly bestow a gentle touch on the shoulder of either individual. This gesture will effectively demonstrate your confidence and admiration for that individual, thus leaving a favorable final impression prior to their confirmation or rejection of your proposal.

Tenderly touch their arm or knee—This NLP technique is frequently employed by therapists and grief counselors as a means of conveying their empathy, care, or genuine investment in an individual's welfare. Take, for instance, the scenario where an individual has entrusted you with the revelation that they have been encountering contemplations of self-harm in recent times. In addition to other recommendations, it is advisable to propose that they seek assistance from a qualified professional. While expressing your sentiment, consider gently resting your hand upon their arm or knee. This will effectively communicate a perception of apprehension, comprehension, and compassion. A person who experiences these sentiments in a challenging circumstance like this is apt to be more susceptible to being persuaded to heed your proposal.

I would like to offer a piece of advice: exercise your utmost discretion when employing this method. Assess your circumstances and respond appropriately—ensuring that your communication does not cause any discomfort to the recipient. It will solely disturb a connection and restrict an individual's capacity to be influenced.

Narcissism

Narcissism is a personality defect that is marked by egotistic veneration of an elusive self-image, frequently resulting in the pursuit of self-indulgence and vanity, often at the detriment of others. Narcissistic individuals frequently exhibit an inflated perception of their own importance, a sense of entitlement, and an insatiable need for attention, even in the absence of any noteworthy accomplishments. They often strive to be regarded as superior, despite lacking the qualifications to support such a claim, and possess an exaggerated view of their achievements and talents. These individuals often become consumed by fantasies of success, power, and perfection, while simultaneously belittling those whom they deem inferior and associating exclusively with those who share their elevated status. They anticipate special treatment, irrespective of merit, and demonstrate a distinct lack of empathy towards the suffering of others. Furthermore, they consistently demand that the world centers around their desires and display adeptness in manipulating others to achieve their objectives.

Narcissistic individuals are excessively enamored with their self-concept to the extent that they are incapable of discerning the distinction between the internalized image they have constructed of themselves and the actual reality of their being. As a result of this, they frequently struggle to acknowledge or respond positively to criticism or being informed of their misconduct, as they demonstrate an incapacity to accept or process critical feedback. They may also take offense when they are afforded equal treatment as others, as they firmly believe in their entitlement to exceptional treatment at all times. They employ the strategy of aggression to diminish individuals in an effort to present themselves in a superior manner. They are lacking self-control, thus it is outside the realm of their capabilities to govern their emotions and actions. They also face substantial difficulties when it comes to managing stress and adjusting to change. However, despite the façade of superiority exhibited by individuals with Narcissistic traits, their behavior is rooted in a profound underlying insecurity and concealed humiliation that arises when they confront the reality of their imperfections. And as they frequently fail to obtain what they desire from the world, they gradually descend into introspection, being confronted by their own shortcomings and inability to overcome them and their delusions, until they ultimately succumb to the precipice of despair. In order to comprehensively grasp the true nature of narcissism and its potential to inflict harm upon its victims, it is imperative to delve into the narrative of Narcissus, the legendary Greek prince from whom this character derives its name.

The tale of Narcissus

According to the mythology, there existed a remarkably attractive and enchanting Greek prince by the name of Narcissus. Despite being both attractive and charismatic, this Prince was excessively engrossed in the ambitions of attaining great achievements upon ascending the throne - the conquest of multiple kingdoms, the triumph in numerous wars, the pursuit of an ideal consort, and perhaps even the aspiration for eternal life. His preoccupations scarcely allowed him to allocate time for interpersonal connections, frequently finding himself sitting contemplatively for extended periods along the banks of the river, consumed by his fantasies. Due to the prince's notable physical attractiveness, numerous women approached him in their finest attire and made advances towards him, seeking to establish a connection with him. However, despite the beauty and charm possessed by these women, Prince Narcissus showed no interest in any of them, frequently disregarding their presence as none of them met his exacting standards for his ideal woman. These women frequently experienced deep emotional distress, yet the majority of them abandoned the pursuit of engaging with him. However, there existed a Nymph by the name of Echo who harbored such deep affection for Prince narcissus that she persisted in her devotion to him. She was extremely enamored with him to the extent that she couldn't relinquish her feelings. However, regardless of all her earnest efforts to win his favor, Prince Narcissus remained resolute and unaffected. With each dismissal, the nymph Echo experienced immense anguish and anguish due to her inability to cease her affections for the object of her desire. And so, on a certain day when her sufferings became unbearable, she made her way to the revered temple and beseeched the deities, 'Oh benevolent gods of retribution, I implore you to grant Narcissus the awareness of the profound agony inflicted by unrequited love.' "Kindly convey to him the immense anguish I have endured." And the deities affirmed that her plea would be granted. Therefore, the deity of retribution assumed control.

Prince Narcissus was situated near the field adjacent to the riverbank, engrossed in contemplation of the forthcoming encounter, eagerly anticipating Echo's presence. She positioned herself at a distance and spoke to the deities, expressing, 'May Prince Narcissus develop affection for the initial individual he encounters.' In that very moment, Prince Narcissus proceeded towards the riverside and gazed into its depths. He beheld a reflection of himself and became enamored with the mirrored image. He desired to fully embody the image and therefore submerged himself in the river thereafter.

This narrative provides a profound psychological exploration of the essence of narcissism and illuminates the inherent proclivity of narcissistic individuals towards self-destruction. Narcissism pervades our daily existence and manifests itself in our commonplace pursuits, such as cultural expressions and social discourse. Narcissism is observed in significant positions within society, such as parenthood and leadership. To gain a more profound comprehension of how the narcissistic behavior of individuals impacts others, it is imperative to acquire an understanding of the various manifestations of narcissism.

Choose a subject

Consider an individual whose physical appearance closely aligns with your desired aesthetic, using the weight loss scenario as an analogy. It is advisable to select an individual who has consistently maintained such physical condition over an extended duration. A frequently addressed topic pertains to athletes, given their tendency to adhere to proper nutrition and employ efficient weight loss regimens.

Watch

After selecting a subject, proceed to conduct research on the individual. Direct your attention towards their capability to reduce or decrease. There exists a multitude of online resources such as YouTube or Vimeo that you may utilize for the purpose of conducting searches. Frequently, athletes are subjected to interviews on various platforms such as blogs and videos where they divulge the methods they employ to maintain their physical fitness.

Seeking the confidential information

Witness the conduct exhibited by the individual. Please observe and make note of the manner in which the health programs are being implemented. Additionally, seek out specific attributes that set the subject apart from others.

- What kind of linguistic expression does he employ?

- What are his principles or ideologies?

- What are his values?

- What is his physical makeup?

You are identifying the unique characteristic that sets apart the individual you are representing as a model. Take a moment for introspection and discern the inherent attributes that were conspicuous.

Once the X Factor has been identified, proceed to arrange the information in a coherent manner that is comprehensible to facilitate emulation or adaptation. Conduct an experiment to verify that the intended outcomes are attained.

Engage in this activity on a daily basis, or at the very least, several times per week. Upon implementing these principles into your daily life for a period of approximately 30 days, either you or those in your vicinity will discern notable improvements in your demeanor, outlook, and physical presentation.

What are the mechanisms behind the influences of Mind Control and Neuro-Linguistic Programming (NLP) on romantic relationships?

Love and relationships are pervasive elements of everyday existence. Affection and interpersonal connections encompass various spheres, including familial, marital, friendly, and professional relationships. To obtain a comprehensive comprehension of love and relationships, it is imperative to initially grasp the intricacies of social institutions. This entails comprehending the locations and mechanisms by which these relationships and feelings of love occur. The establishment of a deep emotional connection is crucial prior to embarking on a relationship, which is a matter deserving sincere consideration.

In order for love to flourish, it is necessary for a genuine connection to be established. This implies the presence of a consistently harmonious setting where individuals can come together and develop their unique connections. To exemplify this point, it can be observed that companionship arises from individuals residing in close proximity to one another. In addition, it is imperative that individuals, be it two or more, harbor shared objectives or, at the very least, mutual interests in order to foster a bond. Furthermore, mutual ideas hold significant importance in the establishment and cultivation of a genuine friendship. Friendship consequently assumes a familial nature, wherein they offer support, counsel, and guidance. Establishing and nurturing friendships is a crucial aspect of an individual's life, as the absence of such connections can result in social isolation and a perception of being solitary.

Marriage constitutes an additional social bond predicated on affection and emotional connection. Matrimony is a sacred union between two individuals. It is widely acknowledged that this holds significant importance in an individual's life. The journey of matrimony commences with a foundation of friendship, progressing towards a deepening connection that culminates in the union of two individuals in the sacred institution of marriage, where they commit to a lifelong partnership. The aforementioned assertion does not hold true for every marital relationship. Matrimony is both straightforward and intricate owing to the integration of two individuals harboring divergent viewpoints and approaches. Disputes between marital partners, while customary as a result of their contrasting characteristics, serve to nourish the vitality of the marriage, in stark contrast to scenarios where spouses possess similar traits.

Family constitutes an additional bond, embodying affection and love. Family is formed through the institutions of matrimony, biological lineage, as well as the act of legal adoption. A family can occasionally be bothersome, yet they consistently remain a source of support in times of solitude or absence of others.

They provide unwavering assistance to individuals at all times and in all matters. This can pertain to the physical, mental, emotional, and financial aspects. The institution of family holds great significance in the lives of individuals. It takes precedence in numerous respects. It serves as the foundation for one's native tongue, etiquette, and can also encompass religious practices for certain individuals. It constitutes the initial phase of socialization that individuals undergo during their formative years.

Another venue for social interaction is the professional setting of an individual's place of employment. An individual's workplace facilitates extensive social interaction with various individuals. Despite its formal nature, work still fosters interpersonal connections. In certain professional environments, interpersonal relationships may culminate in expressions of affection, companionship, and in certain instances, even matrimonial commitments between co-workers. Employment provides individuals with a feeling of security. Colleagues provide invaluable support amidst the challenges of the work environment, and the shared professional context often fosters meaningful friendships. Companions provide crucial support in navigating various challenges, while colleagues possess a comprehensive understanding of significant aspects of one's daily experiences. The workplace serves as an excellent environment for interpersonal interactions.

The synergy between NLP and mind control is evident when it comes to matters of love. Interpersonal bonds and romantic affection are predetermined by cognitive processes. In order for them to function effectively, it is imperative that the mindset is satisfactory. There is a widely held belief that love and interpersonal relationships serve as catalysts for personal transformation. Individuals experience an increased level of sensitivity, openness, and intimacy with their partners and acquaintances. Love possesses an enduring quality, and there exists a perception within certain individuals that it engenders a lack of rationality, not in the literal sense found within literature, but rather in terms of thought and behavior. Love generates feelings of insecurity and heightened sensitivity, consequently exerting an impact on the routine of one's life. Natural Language Processing and the manipulation of thoughts have an impact on the human psyche consistently and without exception. Love has the capacity to alter the cognitive processes and internal framework of the mind.

Navigating the complexities of love and relationships can be challenging yet also offer intriguing opportunities for personal growth. Interpersonal connections foster unity and promote increased proximity among individuals. This has the potential to be found in various locations. It is imperative to engage with individuals intermittently, as one cannot endure existence in isolation. Relationships and love perpetually influence the human mind. The mental attitude of an individual who is experiencing romantic affection exhibits optimism and contentment towards life. Therefore, love and interpersonal connections bring about a profound sense of happiness and fulfillment in individuals. Love is a significant element that permeates the lives of all individuals. Tasks become more manageable and infused with vibrancy.

Simple Agoraphobia NLP Exercises

Agoraphobia is characterized as the most distressing phobia known. It is strongly correlated with the occurrence of panic attacks. There is a commonly held misperception that agoraphobia simply refers to the fear of being in open spaces. It surpasses mere that. Those afflicted by this specific phobia experience an intense apprehension regarding the relinquishment of control, which leads them to limit their activities to a physically enclosed or protected environment. Consequently, apart from discerning the root cause of this phobia, it is imperative to cultivate a sense of composure within oneself, particularly in settings or circumstances where exerting authority is unattainable. Although it is common for individuals to feel some level of unease when confronted with uncontrollable situations, individuals with agoraphobia exhibit heightened levels of concern that extend beyond normal thresholds and escalate to the point of experiencing panic attacks. As an illustration, the majority of individuals feel at ease in public settings, whereas individuals with agoraphobia do not experience such comfort and consequently refrain from spending time or socializing in public spaces. Thankfully, the utilization of NLP can be utilized to alleviate symptoms and treat agoraphobia. Presented herein is a straightforward exercise to achieve this objective.

Define Your Outcome

This marks the initial stage. Articulating your desired outcome may appear self-evident, given that the primary objective of this endeavor is to alleviate agoraphobia. Nevertheless, it is crucial to bear in mind that an outcome should be perceived not as something undesirable, but rather as something one wishes to articulate with a positive connotation. Hence, commence by documenting your desired expression in a constructive manner and consider the emotional impact that will accompany its accomplishment. In the event of uncertainty regarding your desired outcome, envision progressing towards a positive objective and record it in written form as an alternative approach.

Visualization

Proceeding to step 2 entails engaging in a process of mental imagery to apprehend the situational stimuli responsible for inducing this phobic response. Nevertheless, you must consider it from an objective standpoint. As an illustration, one could envision themselves seated on a park bench within a public recreational area or occupying the role of a projectionist within a cinema venue. The key strategy at play here entails visualizing oneself from the perspective of an observer via the medium of a camera lens. Immerse yourself mentally in the triggering scenario and depict it as a silent monochrome film on the projected screen. If this evokes any emotional difficulties, consider envisioning yourself as a spectator to the projection. This serves to establish a certain degree of detachment from the scene and its consequential emotional impacts. Conduct multiple iterations of this exercise until you are able to detach any emotional response from the scene. Observe the unfolding of this visual scenario on the simulated platform, and contemplate the desired qualities or capabilities that your virtual representation should possess. It would be beneficial if the attributes were ones that could assist in effectively managing the triggering situation. For instance, if your agoraphobia stems from a diminished sense of self-assurance, it is imperative that your visual representation exudes a significant amount of confidence. As you execute this task, envision the version of yourself among the spectators imparting various qualities, such as confidence, to the portrayal of your persona on the screen. Please observe the impact that this has on the representation of yourself being displayed on the screen. Does the individual undergo alterations in their emotional and physical demeanor? Continue performing the aforementioned step until the visual representation of yourself on the display possesses all the necessary attributes to effectively manage the given situation that may potentially prompt a reaction. Observe the transformation of your newfound self as it navigates the circumstances that prompt a particular response. Does the scene change? What is the response of the persona depicted on the screen? Examine and replicate the attributes of the visual representation within yourself. Please execute the activity repeatedly at your discretion.

Develop Exceptional Communication Skills Through Neuro-Linguistic Programming (NLP)

Neuro-linguistic programming, also known as NLP, is a highly influential psychological framework that individuals who possess a strong inclination towards communication and persuasion can employ to enhance their ability to convince others. Having a comprehensive understanding of how individuals communicate allows you to discern the underlying framework of communication, whether it be through face-to-face interactions, telephone conversations, or any other technological channels such as email, text messaging, or online chatting.

Communication

Rapport

Rapport ensues when individuals harmonize with one another, sharing a common wavelength, demonstrating a clear comprehension and empathetic response to the ideas expressed or the perspective from which the other person is speaking. In a condition of such nature, the transmission of information manifests heightened efficacy and authenticity, as the involved individuals exhibit a mutual sense of trust.

The conventional approach that Neuro-Linguistic Practitioners employ in order to achieve this empathic state consists of the following methods:

Mirroring

Entails the act of being cognizant of the gestures and mannerisms, as well as the significant words (trance words), employed by the speaker; endeavoring to subsequently provide the speaker with feedback on their conveyed personal values. Individuals have confidence in themselves, and the greater your ability to embody their essence and serve as a mirror, the more likely they are to place their faith in you.

Please be advised that mirroring is not synonymous with being a replica. It must be subtly unobtrusive, almost undetectable yet discernible to the individual's subconscious.

Engaging in Guiding and Influencing

Pacing entails the display of an understanding and empathy towards the other individual's perspective, which can be achieved by acknowledging verifiable aspects of their present circumstances.

Leading entails firmly grasping another individual's hand and guiding them towards the desired destination.

The general pattern is as follows:

Maintain a steady pace, maintaining a steady pace, maintaining a steady pace, and taking the lead. Subsequently, it evolves into Pace, Pace, Lead, Lead. Over time, it transforms into a sequence of Pace, Lead, Lead, Lead.

Suppose you are an individual desiring to initiate acquaintance with the captivating lady you encounter at the shopping center—how can we implement this underlying concept?

Hello, I realize that this may seem unexpected (P) and perhaps unconventional (P), given our unfamiliarity with one another (P). Therefore, may I kindly inquire about your name? (L)

As the level of rapport strengthens, the necessity of using pacing statements diminishes, enabling one to employ more subtle leading techniques. One illustration could be:

So, you are patiently awaiting the arrival of a companion? Excellent! Allow us to proceed to that designated location (L), kindly provide me with further details regarding your background (L), and please inform your friend via text message of your current whereabouts (L).

That serves as a mere illustration, and the identical structure may be employed in various contexts such as business operations, resolving familial disputes, negotiating a more favorable transaction for a vehicle, and so forth.

Sensory Channels of VAKOG (Visual/Auditory/Kinesthetic/Olfactory/Gustatory)

Every individual possesses distinctive characteristics and primarily communicates through any of these sensory channels.

Photographers and painters demonstrate a penchant for visual artistic expression, while musicians possess a remarkable ability to evoke emotions through auditory compositions. Dancers and actors embody kinetic artistry, while perfume designers exhibit an aptitude for olfactory aesthetics. Chefs, on the other hand, manifest their creativity through gastronomic mastery.

The preferred channel varies based on the subject matter at hand. Nonetheless, in order to enhance the influence and ensure that the message is effectively received, it should primarily be directed towards the channel that the recipient is most receptive to.

The resolution remains constant. To commence, you proceed by ascertaining the additional attributes of individuals. If one possesses a comprehensive understanding of generalizations, that is precisely what holds significance. Moreover, it facilitates expediently uncovering the manner in which other inquiries are resolved.

Subsequently, utilize your established patterns in this manner, resulting in highly favorable outcomes. This is the manner in which one should engage in conversation with them. If one is capable of effectively engaging in such discourse, it exemplifies their cognitive approach.

They will possess precise knowledge on how to apply pressure to their buttocks. You will gain precise comprehension of their sentiments and anticipated actions.

That constitutes the entirety of the requirements to effectively communicate in a specific language. It possesses the capacity to exert an impact on particular subjects, and subsequently, it is indubitably accurate. During an ordinary discourse, one has the potential to alter their perspectives and thoughts.

Strategic decision-making: techniques for making informed choices leading to favorable outcomes

The most straightforward approach to acquiring knowledge on performing tasks or inquiring about them is through the utilization of a technique known as 'emotional triggers.' Allow me to elaborate on this matter. Are you aware of the potential outcomes that may arise when he or she is in a specific state? It is highly probable that the appropriate course of action is taken in order to ascertain the potential mental deterioration of an individual. Under such circumstances, she is unable to arrive at a sound decision and assessment. Hence, it can be observed that the majority of individuals tend to make purchasing decisions driven by emotions, yet subsequently seek to rationalize their choices through the lens of affection. I am confident that you are capable of elucidating my current statement.

What steps can be taken when contemplating the phenomenon of brainwashing? It\\\'s very simple. If one desires to engage in self-improvement, all that needs to be done is to pinpoint a query to which the individual is susceptible and proceed with articulating one's viewpoint freely and confidently. The inquiry regarding whether the decision will be in your favor shall remain unanswered. Allow me to relay a message to you. They are aware that humor evokes laughter and brings good fortune upon them. Nonetheless, owing to its nature as a manifestation of self-impairment, it may be feasible to induce a state of partial paralysis, as the restoration of rationality proves to be a challenge.

This statement is widely publicized as a method of influencing individuals to purchase or reach a decision. Nevertheless, I respectfully request to adopt this morally upright approach.

Given the significance of this inquiry, creators of the Internet have begun to comprehend the appropriate response. Numerous manufacturers actively seek out various elements that can be utilized to persuade their clientele. In the forthcoming chapter, I shall illustrate the precise controls employed, which possess such formidable efficacy that they empower you to determine the methodology behind your decision-making.

The union is highly prosperous. Indeed, I can assert that it has a significant impact on my figures. Numerous marketing professionals employ this principle when expressing their viewpoint, duly elucidating its presence within their sales letters and videos. They engage in this practice with the intention of ensuring that you possess a spacious residence while forging a connection between your product and high-priced components. I desire for your assertion to be: "Upon purchasing this product, it is possible to acquire a splendid residence and access sports amenities."

The partnership principle is remarkably effective to the extent that customers are unaware of the unfolding process. In order to utilize it appropriately, it is desirable for your clients to optimize the benefits offered by your product. Present visuals depicting the accurate outcomes generated by your product, followed by the realization of obtaining the precise results. It is of utmost importance and functions with catastrophic consequences.

The subsequent issue at hand is the necessity to engage in a process of ingraining desirable thoughts and ideas into the minds of your esteemed clientele. It is vital to recognize that individuals often make purchasing decisions based on specific components rather than merely considering the entire product line. One can enumerate all the rational and logical justifications for why your product is a favorable choice, however, the ultimate indicators of excellence lie in its merits. If the appropriate keys are pressed, all will be in order and the customer shall be assured of receiving reimbursement for their purchased item.

In order to elicit an emotional response, it is crucial to provide an accurate portrayal of the emotions experienced by your prospective clientele. What makes you work? What are your expectations for your product and for your life in general? When individuals possess the entitlement to receive criticism, it impairs the customers' capacity to engage in rational deliberation on the subject matter.

Furthermore, it is imperative to employ these two methodologies in conjunction. Ensure that the chosen selection accurately portrays the intended emotional facets when utilizing the function. This endeavor exemplifies great accomplishment and promises to yield remarkable outcomes. Nevertheless, given the considerable potency of this substance, I strongly advise you to employ these capsules.

Many individuals possess a keen interest in acquiring the ability to exert discipline over their own physical disposition. Public and private entities, including government and various institutions, have undertaken research and deliberations to address additional inquiries aimed at comprehending the appropriate methods of verifying the successful execution of these measures. The concepts of brainwashing, cognition, indoctrination, and related issues pertain to individual agency and the manner in which individuals exercise their own decision-making capacity. The crux of the matter is to employ a multitude of approaches to convince an individual or collective to adopt a specific stance or assume a particular role. Throughout the years, these approaches have been employed in various manners, primarily – albeit not exclusively – due to ethical considerations.

Initially, it was believed that its usage was confined solely to totalitarian governments across the globe. To guarantee that they address a regulation that culminates in violence, they repress anything that is resolved through brutality. Furthermore, mechanisms are employed to communicate information that is deemed applicable to both a captive combatant and a prisoner of war, in order to guarantee adherence to state regulations. Hence, it was feasible to address the inquiry regarding the emergence of the question regarding whether the query arises as to whether the matter arises in terms of the question of the query. If the inquiry prompts contemplation on whether or not to inquire about the matter, the query pertains to the likelihood of inquiry eliciting a response regarding the statements the prisoner ought to make, until it is determined that this indeed holds true. Additionally, they would require them to articulate their perspectives in writing. Naturally, an alternative was also employed, as its guarantee cannot be assured.

Undoubtedly, it is crucial to possess the knowledge and proficiency to effectively employ one's command, particularly in specific circumstances often referred to as cults. Frequently, these groups consist of highly charismatic individuals who possess extensive knowledge. One of the justifications for extending support to these followers is when they originate from insufficiently qualified households and acquaintances who do not align with the proper faith. While there are varying perspectives, it is imperative that you possess the liberty to express yourself and engage actively in your forthcoming existence.

The final example is affirmative. Indeed, it is possible to cleanse your mind if you are confident in your improvement. One potential approach is to encounter challenges. Compose your desired aspirations in written form, and subsequently, during subsequent instances, articulate the contents pertaining to the query regarding your certainty.

If you are inclined to make a decision, kindly communicate with me, expressing, 'I intend to pursue that course,' and inform him that it will involve persuasion, reiterating the same. Engage in this activity consistently, and you will observe a gradual transformation in your perception of self. By virtue of its capacity for reproduction, the written content permeates the depths of your subconscious and necessitates an assessment of its veracity in terms of specific attributes. It can be inferred, echoing the sentiments of Michael Jordan, that there exists a correctness in one's ability to articulate thoughts through the written and spoken word, and to comprehend written text. Moreover, Jordan's perspective encompasses an understanding of how specific elements will be delineated in forthcoming narratives. This pertains to the present situation.

It is of utmost importance to possess the knowledge and abilities to regulate one's thoughts and mental faculties, whether for virtuous or malevolent purposes. Presumably, your justifications for the potential enhancements it can bring to your life. Utilizing hypnosis proves to be an exceedingly proficient technique for altering one's cognitions that have been formulated within specific locales or domains.

"Would it be advisable to consider the application of hypnosis as a form of mind control?

Brainwashing has an astonishing historical trajectory. If we contemplate the query, it is plausible to state that even the operatives of the Central Intelligence Agency who are driven to address the question, whether they ought to be concerned about it, whether they should attend to it, or whether they are mandated to safeguard their well-being. Therefore, is it imperative to cleanse the mind? Fundamentally, I believe it could be ascertained in that manner. In conclusion, the purpose of hypnosis and control is to exert an influence over the subject, which aligns precisely with the desired outcome. In a broader context, I believe it surpasses mere hypnosis and engenders enduring impacts.

Although government representatives may be incentivizing the implementation of navigation practices, it is uncertain whether their actions are deemed accurate. Cult leaders have effectively exercised authority over their adherents for an extended duration, molding their thoughts and behaviors in a manner that distances them from rational comprehension. Techniques employed include hypnosis love bombing, reinforcement of guilt, exploitation through emotional exposure, gradually fostering dependence on the cult for self-esteem, and relinquishing decision-making authority regarding their behavior to the cult.

Nevertheless, in order to arrive at sound judgments, brainwashing typically addresses the query of whether selection and nurturing amount to a manifestation thereof. Essentially, the individual who is being manipulated is placed in an intensified state that effectively determines whether or not he has any opportunity to evade or elude.

What are your thoughts regarding the utilization of hypnosis for mind control? Many individuals may assert that it is conceivable to genuinely comprehend your capabilities, however, it is plausible that an individual could have the chance to thoroughly unveil all the implications that align with your specific circumstances.

Please be aware that possessing knowledge of this confidential form of hypnosis is not a prerequisite for establishing your own following. In reality, that is one of the factors contributing to these issues. It is probable that you will acquire the ability to exert influence over the operation without necessitating any intervention. Employing this method of influencing, known as "influence," may occasionally be regarded as challenging.

This phenomenon arises primarily from the prevalence of this type of influence within the technology we employ. The individuals upon whom you apply conversational hypnosis will not be rendered passive, but there is no doubt that hypnotic techniques indeed yield results. They effectively surmount a considerable amount of resistance, particularly when attempting to influence someone to do something they genuinely desired to do in the first place, thereby assisting you in achieving your objectives.

Acquiring the skill to manage methodologies holds practical value when effectively employed, yet may pose hazards if entrusted to inappropriate individuals.

While certain individuals employ them for the purpose of personal growth, others exhibit no reservations when it comes to utilizing them in a manner that jeopardizes your well-being. Do not permit yourself to be manipulated. Continue reading to gain further insight into these approaches.

"Cognitive Manipulation Method:

This results in a source of frustration.

Numerous individuals currently engage in acts of assistance, aiding others, preserving recollections, and even experiencing life. Occasionally, they endeavor to assist individuals in discovering more about their own identities.

Unrelated to the discovery of a viable solution. Indeed, numerous individuals have attested to the efficacy of hypnosis sessions.

How NLP Works

Have you ever experienced a period in your life wherein you desired to modify negative conduct and engage in a completely different endeavor, only to discover that you ultimately reverted to your previous habits?

If you have ever pondered the rationale behind our perpetual repetition of ingrained patterns, it can be attributed to the overpowering influence of restrictive behaviors and detrimental emotions, which exert a greater force than our conscious cognition. Given that our unconscious minds are responsible for the generation and storage of patterns and habits, it becomes necessary to effect change at the unconscious level.

If we were able to simply assert "I hereby renounce this behavior immediately," the services of therapists would be rendered unnecessary.

Undesired convictions and conducts have been acquired and ingrained within the depths of the unconscious mind. These items no longer fulfill their purpose and therefore require replacement. During your juvenile years, it is possible that you developed a dislike for peanut butter due to the presence of a sibling with a peanut allergy. Peanut butter was never present within the household, thereby depriving you of the experience of its taste. You were brought up with the belief that peanut butter was unappealing or detrimental to your well-being. This information was assimilated into the unconscious realm, resulting in your ongoing unfamiliarity with the taste of peanut butter. This constitutes an inherent automated response, impervious to conscious alteration. They are alterable solely at the level of the unconscious mind.

This holds true when it comes to convictions. It is possible that an entrenched belief, which originated during your formative years, could impede your progress presently. For instance, consider the statement "I consistently fail to complete any task I begin." This perspective is solely based on a personal belief. This statement lacks veracity and has the potential to be altered unconsciously into a notion that could enhance the quality of your life.

Frequently, individuals are unaware of the manner and reasons behind their actions. This is where Natural Language Processing (NLP) becomes relevant. It will facilitate your comprehension and enable you to modify your behaviors and reactions that are no longer effective, thereby fostering a more comprehensive and fulfilling existence. Seize the opportunity to embrace your existence and actively engage in living it to its fullest potential.

It has the potential to significantly transform your life.

Natural Language Processing has the potential to assist individuals in addressing their fears. This statement does not solely pertain to fears associated with creatures or insects. This pertains to apprehensions such as social anxiety or glossophobia. NLP has the potential to cultivate self-assurance by fostering the conviction that one possesses the courageous ability to address an audience. It has the ability to uplift you by conveying that your significance within society is noteworthy, distinguishing you from being merely an anonymous presence amidst a multitude. Natural Language Processing (NLP) has the capacity to alleviate symptoms of depression or enhance one's self-esteem levels.

NLP has the potential to aid in the attainment of your objectives. Through the use of NLP, individuals have the ability to identify their shortcomings and consequently rewire their cognitive processes in a manner that promotes self-empowerment and facilitates their triumph over these weaknesses. A significant number of contemporary athletes are adopting the practice of Neuro-Linguistic Programming (NLP) as a means to enhance their skills and achieve remarkable success within their respective domains. They are not only exerting physical effort, but also challenging their cognitive abilities to reach new pinnacles. Consider the potential achievements that may be realized through the application of committed resolve and the diligent utilization of the aforementioned strategies.

Natural Language Processing (NLP) has the potential to assist with the enhancement of one's personality as well. It has the capacity to impart the ability to comprehend and empathize with others. It has the capacity to impart knowledge on empathetic comprehension of others' emotions and sentiments. It is imperative that you begin to demonstrate a higher level of respect towards others and actively encourage and inspire them to pursue their aspirations. Others may perceive a transformation in your demeanor, resulting in an increased propensity to draw the attention of acquaintances or individuals seeking your company due to the positive energy you emanate. Certain individuals may regard you as a figure to emulate. Considering this aspect, it is plausible that you could initiate the process of instructing or mentoring others. They may express gratitude for your assistance in attaining their objectives.

Utilizing Emotional Freedom Technique to Address Restrictive Beliefs

The Emotional Freedom Technique (EFT) demonstrates efficacy in addressing negative emotions stemming from restrictive beliefs. It can be asserted that EFT serves as a psychological equivalent to acupuncture. Acupuncture employs the utilization of needles to activate around 365 specific points located within the 12 primary meridians of the human body.

Conversely, EFT relies solely on the utilization of fingers, tapping on approximately 7-18 designated points along the same 12 meridians, adhering to a specific sequence and rhythm.

A disturbance in the body's energy system is the underlying factor that gives rise to all adverse emotions. If the interruption persists, it has the potential to result in psychological anguish and ultimately bodily ailment. EFT utilizes precise tapping techniques on specific meridian points across the face and body to restore equilibrium to disrupted energy. Upon eliminating the energy obstructions, we simultaneously relinquish the detrimental emotional states.

As previously discussed, belief is invariably accompanied by an emotional response. One feasible approach to address the adverse emotions that stem from constraining beliefs is through the utilization of Electronic Funds Transfer (EFT). What are the sensations you experience when envisioning yourself possessing a slender and perfect physique? Do you experience feelings of antipathy, rage, sorrow, envy, or apprehension? In this literary work, I shall employ the illustration of the apprehension associated with potential loss. Afraid of losing weight? Do individuals exist who exhibit apprehension towards losing weight? It may be surprising, but there are indeed individuals who exemplify this description. For instance, there was an artist of ample build who harbored a fear of shedding weight. He believed that possessing a slender physique would diminish his level of popularity.

The emotions you experience exert significant influence over your subsequent actions and conduct. The outcome is directly influenced by one's emotions. If one harbors a fear of weight loss, achieving weight loss will not be attainable. You need not justify or rationalize your emotions. If you have an aversion to weight loss, there is no need to ponder over the reasons behind your aversion. By relinquishing your aversion to shedding pounds, you will consequently achieve weight loss. It has come to my attention that through the utilization of EFT, it is not necessary for us to ascertain the limiting belief. Further exploration into the depths of the subconscious mind is unnecessary. We must solely ascertain the extent of the adverse emotional impact caused by the constraining belief. The greater the intensity of the emotion, the more profound its impact on us. Through the application of EFT, it is possible to effectively mitigate, if not entirely diminish, the intensity of adverse emotions. Once we relinquish the negative emotions, we simultaneously let go of our emotional bond to that constraining belief. Upon effectively resolving and liberating ourselves from negative emotions, the constraining belief will cease to exert influence over our behaviors.

Our initial step involves assessing the SUD intensity. SUD denotes Subjective Units of Discomfort, alternatively referred to as Subjective Units of Distress. SUD is employed for the purpose of tracking the advancement.

We quantify the subjective unit of distress on a scale ranging from 0 to 10. Zero denotes a state of neutrality or absence of issues, whereas ten signifies the most unfavorable circumstance. The objective of Emotional Freedom Technique (EFT) is to effectively diminish the intensity of emotional states to a level of complete absence.

Experience the magnitude of your emotional state, and quantify it using the Subjective Units of Distress (SUD) scale. There is no need for you to feel perplexed when making a decision. If you are unable to ascertain the correct numerical value, simply make an estimation and proceed accordingly.

EFT Tapping Points

Prior to proceeding, it is important that we familiarize ourselves with the EFT tapping points. There are three key aspects to consider:

- A few of the connection points feature dual points. An instance of this is exemplified by the presence of dual loci, specifically on both the right and left sides of Eye Brow. It is sufficient to tap either of the twin points, without any preference as to which side is tapped. Furthermore, it is possible to alternate positions by touching these points.

- Many novice individuals are concerned about whether they have accurately selected the appropriate location. The action of tapping is executed using two fingertips, namely the index and the middle fingertips. By adopting this approach, you will be able to encompass a broader expanse and guarantee the accuracy of your tapping onto the precise location. You have the option to tap with either hand, however, I recommend using your dominant hand.

You execute approximately 7 taps on each point. However, it is unnecessary to meticulously tally the number of taps applied, as a range of 3 to 7 taps is sufficient in most cases, with the exception of Sore Spot and Gamut Point.

AUTUMN LEAVES

A metaphorical representation illustrating the notion of relinquishing the past as a means to embrace the present and future, while encouraging active participation.

Previous, relinquishing

You are leisurely strolling through a forest during a pleasant autumn afternoon. The terrain is adorned with a coating of autumn foliage, emitting a sonorous combination of crackles and rustles as one treads upon it.

Amidst the foliage, a profound azure canopy emerges, presenting a hue of unparalleled depth.

While the accumulation of leaves on the path obscures its visibility, the branches of the trees remain adorned with leaves, displaying hues ranging from a radiant golden yellow to a deep orange and a vibrant red.

One can perceive a gentle coolness in the atmosphere, yet their spirit is embraced by the brilliance emanating from the surrounding hues. One may experience an internal radiance that mirrors the vibrant hues of the foliage. Symbolic of your aspirations, the hue of gold embodies the targets you strive to attain, while the color orange epitomizes the dynamism and vigor that fuels your efforts to reach them. Lastly, the shade of red represents the unwavering strength and determination you draw upon to conquer any uncertainties along your path.

You are continuing in your ambulation; however, there is a noticeable deceleration in your pace. While acknowledging the necessity of making progress, it is equally crucial to occasionally pause and observe our surroundings. You perceive, with growing conviction, that the present moment is one of those instances.

You pause.

This appears to be the most ancient section of the forest. Towering trees loom majestically on both sides, reaching towards the heavens.

The surface of the closest tree trunk is riddled with an intricate network of fissures, and upon closer examination, one can observe the presence of pale green lichen adorning the elevated portions.

The bark displays a fragility that gives the impression of disintegration upon contact. However, upon placing one's hand on the tree, its texture exudes a formidable and unyielding quality akin to that of granite. The fissures serve as conduits of resilience, rather than mere manifestations of vulnerability. Towards the base of the tree, there exist pockets of moss, and you tenderly graze your fingertips upon them. One anticipates the moss to possess a slimy and damp sensation, yet it manifests as dry and feathery upon contact.

As one positions oneself in close proximity to the tree, an impression of antiquity and eternal nature emanates, seemingly conveying a profound revelation via tactile means to the innermost realms of comprehension.

It appears as though the accumulated wisdom of the ancient philosophers, the mythical magicians, and our very own forefathers has been consolidated and safeguarded within the essence of the tree.

You cast your gaze downward towards the trunk of the tree. The tree is fortified and sustained by its robust roots that extend in every direction, resembling sturdy buttresses. It is well-known that the root system of a tree extends to a distance equal to its height. In a fleeting moment of contemplation, one envisions perceiving these roots underground, stretching forth to acquire water and nutrients. As they grow deeper and extend further, they branch out, gradually becoming more delicate in their quest to nourish and support the tree.

One gazes upward and beholds the serene and assured ascent of the branches, mirroring the intricate network of roots that branch out and extend in their quest for the nourishment of sunlight.

Overhead, a bough quivers in the wind, causing a leaf to delicately detach and descend gracefully to the earth below. One more leaf ensues, and another. In a matter of mere weeks, the branches of the tree will become devoid of foliage. Within the realm of one's imagination, it is conceivable to perceive the passage of time as it progresses from the winter to the spring season. One can envision the emergence of buds upon the tree branches, gradually expanding and ultimately unfurling into tender, new leaves. It becomes evident that this transformative process would cease to occur if the tree did not relinquish its previous foliage during the autumn months.

You reflect upon the aspects of your existence that you desire to relinquish: activities that no longer hold appeal, pessimistic thoughts, and any impediments hindering your desired self-actualization.

The tree is undergoing leaf abscission due to its appropriate physiological timing. You have reached the point where you believe it is opportune to relinquish the aspects of your life that you wish to eliminate. And as you experience their gradual detachment, each fragment drifting down in a downward motion, farther from your existence, you find yourself liberated to engage in new pursuits, relish in uplifting thoughts, and mold yourself to your desired state.

A profound sense of liberation permeates your consciousness when you come to the realization that henceforth, the necessity for these things to be present in your life has been eliminated.

Comprehending the Psychosocial Requirements of the marital partner

Dr. Hale extensively conducted research primarily focused on individuals who possess multinational enterprises and exhibit diverse cultural backgrounds.

During one of the training sessions held in the psychological parenting seminar, I prompted the couples to compile a comprehensive inventory of the psychological requirements necessary for the fulfillment and satisfaction of both husbands and wives. Following the aforementioned assessment of these requirements, I instructed them to convene within a designated space in order to consolidate the list, eliminating any redundant entries and amalgamating their responses into key focal points. Likewise, the male individuals within the group were requested to convene and collectively determine the requirements, establishing fundamental shared points accordingly. Therefore, upon arriving at the ultimate outcome, the revelation proved to be profoundly distressing for contemporary psychologists. The psychological requirements of the husband and the necessities of the wife are utterly distinct. Thus, it remains the same. Now, let us proceed to analyze the contrasts. .

Primary Psychological need

The primary psychological requirement of the husband, as per their hierarchy of needs, was intimacy, specifically in the form of sexual relations. Over time, this need transitioned from purely physical satisfaction to a desire for emotional connection and love. They consistently prioritized sexuality, and instances have occurred where women declined to engage in sexual activities in the manner he desired, thereby leading to multiple instances of homicide and manslaughter. The requirement for a spouse is sexual intimacy. That stood as the topmost necessity for the husband in the aforementioned list.

Upon examination of the disparity, it becomes apparent that the foremost requirement listed by men and women is that of emotional fondness. The woman did not prioritize sexual encounters; instead, her focus was on experiencing love and affection. Furthermore, with regards to the occurrence in question, have you happened to have viewed the film titled "Call Center"? In the film, the male protagonist and the female lead encounter each other at the male protagonist's workplace, which happens to be a call center. The woman initially reprimands the young boy for his incorrect billing, thus initiating the formation of their friendship. They initiated their friendship through engagement in quarrels, yet the gentleman displayed remarkable submissiveness and humility. After a series of romantic encounters, the woman ultimately expresses her love for him by extending a proposal, as she experienced a profound sense of ease and contentment in his presence. For women, the transition is from love to sex, rather than the reverse. That elucidates the complete disparity in psychological needs between males and females.

Secondary Psychological need

Turning to the second requirement, the husband expressed his concern that the woman failed to acknowledge him as the "head of the household" and did not recognize his role as a family leader. The gentleman states that by merely acknowledging the woman as the leader and authority figure of the household, claiming that she is the highest authority in the domestic realm, the husband would be willing to fulfill any of her desires or requests. Therefore, the man's second requirement is to be accepted. You acknowledge me as a fellow leader of the household.

The second set of requirements expressed by women differs as well. While men sought recognition of their "leadership," women sought "congenial family ties," whereby men would accept them and their families. For various households, women establish distinct interpretations of the term "family."

For a subset of women, the concept of family encompasses not only the individual, but also her parents. Therefore, she desires for her spouse to assume responsibility for both her and their parents, with the children occasionally serving as the motivation behind her commitment to family. This is how she delineates the conception of family, distinct from the manner in which the majority of men conceive the family. Frequently, the distinction lies in the delineation of "your community and my community", "your kinsfolk and my kinsfolk". This has been the prevailing pattern of events. Once the husband expresses his desire for the wife to acknowledge him as the "head of the household," the wife also seeks the husband's acceptance of her and her "family" in return.

Third Psychological need

The third psychological requirement of the husband is the desire for a companion, a collaborator with whom he can engage in humorous exchanges and engage in recreational activities at his convenience. In the majority of instances, particularly when dealing with my clientele who possess demanding professional commitments. Consider a spouse who is engrossed in professional tasks on his portable computing device. The spouse tends to his nourishment and serves him coffee concurrently. He graciously accepts everything she presents to him, diligently attending to his laptop work without imposing any stipulations. When the husband becomes disinterested in using the laptop, he seeks the company of his wife. During that period, he desires the lady to perform in accordance with his specifications. The gentleman's decision to spend time with the lady is not based on her wishes, but rather on his own boredom. This is why he desires a companion at his disposal, a woman to engage in playful activities with.

Considering the requirements of the woman, she desires a companion with whom she can engage in extended and meaningful conversations. It is talk mate. He is in search of a "companion for recreation" while she is seeking a "companion for conversation". The essence of the matter is that women seek companions with whom they can engage in conversation, particularly when experiencing stress or confronting difficult circumstances. She intends to alleviate the stress by engaging in open communication with her husband, sharing the burden of anxiety together. What is it that she desires? She desires an individual who possesses the ability to lend an attentive ear to her. Although she possesses the capacity to manage the situation, her desire is simply for someone who can lend an ear and actively engage in the conversation. This represents the third psychological requirement of both the husband and the wife.

What Is The Scheduled Commencement Time Of The Presentation?

At what time do you anticipate the commencement of a stage play or musical performance? At what point do the actors initially articulate their lines? Within the prelude of the performance, in the music that is being played? Upon one's arrival at the theatre, perhaps? The response is that it commences at the point of ticket purchase.

What is the designated commencement time for a social gathering with friends in the evening? Upon entering the bar? As you're getting ready? As you are preparing to depart from your workplace?

When will your vacation commence? At what time do you disembark from the aircraft? Alternatively, when would you like to make the reservation?

Why is this? When thoughts arise regarding activities such as a night out, a holiday, or a presentation, it is inevitable that one begins to construct a mental representation or simulation of said experiences. Once the decision is made, your mind immediately initiates the process of preparing you for it. The preparation could encompass contemplating the attendees, envisioning potential scenarios, experiencing anticipation, considering learning objectives, and strategizing logistics.

Our sustenance relies on foreseeing what lies ahead. Our capacity to apprehend balls and trains necessitates a future which mirrors the past; hence, we establish universal principles that remain applicable throughout time. The issue lies in the fact that our future projections are derived from historical occurrences, which, as expressed by financial professionals overseeing your investments, poses a considerable degree of risk.

It is an inherent, innate phenomenon of humanity, and through conscious acknowledgment, one attains heightened mastery.

Prior to taking the podium to address your audience, it is crucial to acknowledge that your communication with them begins well in advance. Consequently, it is imperative that you initiate measures to mold their expectations in favor of achieving your intended objective.

If you were to inquire, a significant number of individuals would assert that the commencement of a presentation occurs when they rise to address the audience.

This statement is not useful due to two main factors:

It intensifies the emphasis on the act of rising, which is the aspect that many individuals tend to evade.

It squanders a significant opportunity to shape the audience's perception and establish their anticipations.

What forms of communication are established with the audience prior to the presentation, which can effectively bolster the delivery of your presentation?

Do you distribute a schedule of topics to be discussed? A joining pack? An email? Every instance presents an occasion to prime the audience in anticipation of your presentation, consequently significantly improving the probability of attaining your desired outcomes.

Providing the audience with a preview of what to anticipate will enable them to appropriately regulate their attentiveness.

Failure to do so may result in their attention being drawn towards information that aligns with their preconceived notions, leading to erratic outcomes at most.

Establish the audience's expectations from the outset of your communication.

Upon rising from your seat, you venture into a hypothetical realm situated at the forefront of the chamber, meticulously crafted by the spectators in attendance. The presence of an audience is contingent upon the presence of a presenter, implying that you are entering a position that awaits your assumption.

Upon entering the premises, you assume authority over the environment, ensuring that you do not, under any circumstances, relinquish control to the audience until you deem it appropriate to do so.

Planning states

What will be the initial state of the audience? Open minded? Curious? Impatient?

Numerous presenters tend to commence their presentations without initially attuning themselves to the current state of the audience. This is an imperative task within the realm of professional communication, commonly referred to as pacing.

Commence by considering the initial condition of the audience. Subsequently, while considering the intended result for the presentation, opt for a beneficial final state that serves the audience's needs. Finally, plan a route.

It is of paramount importance to adopt a pragmatic approach in assessing the initial condition of the audience. While it may be desirable for them to exhibit curiosity, it is important to consider the fact that they may be fatigued and uninterested. Please bear in mind that their initial condition is impartial, devoid of any positive or negative connotation, and is in no way interconnected with you.

The commencement of their condition will be contingent upon not only the events that transpired before their presentation, but also their anticipations concerning the presentation itself, derived from their past encounters. This point holds significant importance as well, serving as a demonstration of the necessity of being aware of the commencement of the presentation.

You may likely perceive this as an extension of the pacing and leading principle, with the initial stage of pacing entailing the establishment of rapport. There is little value in feigning curiosity if the audience is in a critical mindset. Initially, it is imperative to assess their current critical state in order to guide them towards recovery. What is the method by which you accomplish that task? Indeed, would you prefer if I were to attend and deliver the presentation on your behalf?

Presenters lacking the benefit of this approach often initiate their presentations by devising their intended message instead of strategizing how they wish their audience to react. Hence, their presentations tend to resemble transmissions rather than interactive exchanges.

What about technical presentations? Certainly, it can be affirmed that they primarily fulfill the purpose of enlightening or imparting knowledge to the spectators. Once more, what is your desired course of action regarding that information? Agree with it? Make a decision? Understand it? Use it? Misuse it?

The starting point in the design of a presentation is always to consider the outcome for the audience. Once you have acquired this knowledge, the remainder becomes straightforward.

Swish It!

Swish is an immensely potent methodology that necessitates unwavering concentration on the intricacies involved in comprehending and honing this form of art. I will provide comprehensive instruction, leading you systematically through the process of learning. Thoroughly review the instructions before proceeding to execute the methodology.

I kindly request that you relocate to a serene and tranquil environment, devoid of any disruptions or interruptions.

Please ensconce yourself in a comfortable position, gently close your eyes, allow your body to unwind, and inhale deeply.

Once you have reached that mental state, I kindly request that you envision your current circumstances (with the aid of a visual prompt) in which you find yourself in a state of discontentment. As soon as you engage in that activity, your mind will become active and stimulations of various thoughts and images will arise. I would appreciate it if you could endeavour to attain a state of mental and physical relaxation while maintaining steadiness in the primary image. Cultivating a state of mental relaxation will decelerate cognitive processing, allowing for a clearer perception of the principal image. Experience the emotions that are linked to this visual representation.

Alter your current state of mind

Now ponder upon the preferred visual representation along with the corresponding emotions linked to it. This depiction mirrors the desired outcome you seek to attain through your diligent endeavors. Consider the notion that you have surmounted your predicament and currently exist in the desired state you have long yearned for. You will experience a boost in mood and a sense of optimism and joy. I desire for your mind to maintain a state of relaxation, enabling you to visualize this image with utmost clarity.

Disrupt the current state of your mental faculties

Envision, if you will, the experience of witnessing a pair of images displayed upon the vast projection screen within the confines of the Picture Works Factory of your imagination. The initial image serves as the cue (Step 2). The displayed image has been magnified on the screen. The second image corresponds to the image you desire (as indicated in Step 5). The dimensions of this image are quite diminutive, necessitating its placement in the lower right quadrant of the screen.

You are now required to mentally visualize the images. Rapidly reduce the size of your reference image and magnify the intended image. The imperative is to ensure that the envisioned image is vividly depicted within your consciousness. Enhance the brightness and enhance the vibrancy of the colors in this image. Subsequently, amplify the intensity of positive emotions to facilitate the assimilation of both the image and its associated sentiments into the depths of your subconscious. As the cue image diminishes in size, the corresponding emotions linked to it gradually dissipate.

Once more, dispel this mental state by widening your perspective and allowing clarity to permeate your consciousness.

Please proceed to shut your eyes while summoning your cue image and desired image within the realm of your mind's eye. Commence by magnifying the cue image along with its corresponding emotions, subsequently expedite the enlargement of the desired image, while concurrently diminishing the size of the cue image. As positive emotions are revived and reach their zenith. With the intention of maintaining those positive emotions at the forefront of your thoughts, proceed to swiftly manipulate the mental imagery and their respective proportions once more.

Continue performing the swish technique on the two images until the desired image becomes firmly imprinted in your mind, and the cue image becomes closely linked with the associated emotions and sentiments of the desired image. Perform the swish the necessary number of times according to your requirements. Ensure to intermittently disrupt the prevailing state of consciousness to verify the functionality and enduring influence of the swish technique upon your cognitive faculties.

The aforementioned procedure bears a striking resemblance to the example I previously elucidated in our discourse regarding the interplay of your conscious and subconscious faculties. In the preceding chapter, I have explicated the cognitive processes involved when employing the swish technique, whereas in the present chapter, I have provided instructions on how to effectively utilize said technique. It is imperative that one engages in regular practice of the aforementioned steps in order to foster a cognitive association within their subconscious mind, linking negative memories or adverse circumstances with positive emotions and a state of optimism. When experiencing a state of positivity, individuals have a tendency to spontaneously envision positive scenarios within their thoughts, thus initiating a cycle of positivity that permeates their lives.

It is important to bear in mind that achieving mastery in an artistic endeavor entails persistent practice until a flawless execution is attained. Once you have achieved proficiency, it is essential to consistently engage in deliberate practice to attain mastery, thereby reaching a stage where the execution of the skill becomes flawless and errors are eliminated indefinitely. Mastering the proper execution of this NLP methodology will enable you to effectively regulate the generation of visual representations within your Picture Works Factory, thereby linking the desired emotions associated with your target image to the stimulus image. The incorporation of your emotions holds comparable significance within the swish technique, necessitating their acknowledgment.

Chapter Three: Developing Proficiency in the Skill of Provoking Emotional Responses for the Purpose of Influencing

It is possible that you hold the belief that customers typically make purchases only after thoroughly researching the relevant information - however, this perspective is not accurate. In actuality, customers often make decisions based on their instinctual reactions. Having knowledge of this fact can aid in facilitating your ability to exert influence upon them with greater ease.

Have you ever found yourself swayed to contribute a donation to a charitable cause solely upon viewing a digital advertisement depicting the plight of orphaned children, war victims, refugees, and the like? Was the advertisement a reminder of the fortunate circumstances you are presently in, contrasting with the less favorable situation portrayed in the ad? In a short span of time, one may unwittingly retrieve their credit card from their purse and make an unplanned contribution amounting to several hundred dollars.

Indeed, the sentiment of 'guilt' is stirred by a well-executed campaign. You were swayed in your decision-making process due to being led into a heightened state of vulnerability. This serves as a prominent illustration of how companies and salespeople enhance their ability to exert influence by exploiting these deeply felt emotions.

One fundamental truth that warrants recognition is that purchasing decisions are a direct outcome of the emotional disposition of the customer. These emotional changes can be harnessed to your advantage, particularly if your ultimate objective is to become an individual of significant impact or to enhance your sales performance.

7 Techniques for Exploiting Emotional Stimuli

Apprehension (If I do not make a purchase at this moment, I will be in significant trouble).

Jealousy (If I do not make a prompt decision, my competitor will surpass me in performance).

Embarrassment would ensue should I fail to obtain the product at this moment, as it would reflect unfavorably on my reputation.

Desire (If I were to avail of the service at this moment, I undoubtedly stand to be reciprocated)

Acquiring PRIDE at this moment would enhance my intellectual image.

Promoting the well-being of others through timely action on my part manifests altruism.

REMORSE (Should I fail to reach a conclusion, I will undoubtedly experience regret)

Allow me to present a brief illustration:

Fear possesses significant influence, capable of superseding the entirety of one's cognitive processes. The sentiment is responsible for eliciting immediate responses even in the absence of deliberate cognitive processes. Although it may not be the most secure approach to sway individuals, we must acknowledge its significant efficacy. According to the Protection Motivation Theory, individuals are consistently compelled to safeguard themselves against various types of adversities. An excellent illustration of this can be seen in the marketing initiative undertaken by Tuborg (Carlsberg), wherein they strategically exploited the phenomenon known as the 'Fear of Missing Out' and effectively employed the slogan 'Always Say Yes'.

Comprehend the Ideologies of Your Target Consumer Base

The inquiry at present lies in how one can effectively leverage these emotional states to one's benefit. Initial considerations should be given to the utilization of these modifications in cases where a profound comprehension of the customer's personal belief structure is present. The belief system serves as the primary precursor for determining the manifestation of emotions.

Allow us to consider an illustrative scenario: should a prospective client perceive STARBUCKS as the primary contender, it is inevitable that sentiments of both 'admiration' and 'apprehension' will ensue. The sales strategy should be formulated on how to effectively address these emotional challenges and competently compete against a multinational coffee chain franchise.

Alternatively, if Starbucks were to be considered as your prospective client, it would be advisable to strategically tailor your sales approach in a manner that effectively stimulates sentiments of 'pride' and perhaps even 'greed'. This is a situation that necessitates thorough investigation. It is imperative that you ensure a comprehensive comprehension of the present emotional state, as well as the potential fluctuations of these emotions based on the customer's belief system.

An additional illustration pertains to the scenario wherein one endeavors to vend a product or service to the senior executives of the organization. In the majority of instances, given the fiercely competitive nature of the upper management tier, executives are highly averse to committing significant errors that would result in substantial financial losses for the company. When attempting to market a product or service to these professionals, it can be inferred that the element of "apprehension" will undoubtedly influence their decision-making process. If they make a mistake, they could risk losing their position. Now, what actions can be taken to alleviate their apprehension? That is the product you will be offering for sale.

Essential Lessons in Inducing Emotions

The primary determinant you can leverage pertains to the affective ramifications inherent in your proposition. It is imperative to ensure that your products not only offer innovative outcomes to the customer but also possess the ability to revamp previous projects or plans.

It is equally crucial to recognize that individuals must experience a sense of motivation prior to engaging in business with someone. These are the three prevalent human encounters that individuals require prior to expressing their affirmative response to whatever merchandise or service you are endeavoring to market to them.

Assurance – It is crucial for them to have the complete conviction that you possess the necessary qualifications, abilities, and knowledge to fulfill their requirements.

Sense of nurturance - Once individuals perceive that you genuinely prioritize their well-being, they will readily engage in transactions with you.

Trust is crucially important in establishing a solid foundation for successful business relationships. Once individuals are confident that they can place their complete reliance in your integrity and credibility, they will naturally be more inclined to engage in transactions with you.

Focus on Selling the Emotion Rather than the Product!

The satisfaction of your customers' emotional requirements is a valuable asset in the realm of sales. It is imperative to gain a comprehensive comprehension of their application in order to leverage them for your benefit.

By attending to these emotional needs, you will enhance your ability to establish a rapport effortlessly, thereby instilling a sense of confidence and trust in your prospect. To put it succinctly, your emphasis lies in the selling of emotions rather than solely on the products themselves. By appealing to the emotions of your customers, you will have the ability to effectively persuade them to make purchases from you.

Now that you have acquired knowledge regarding the utilization of emotion triggers to enhance your influence, it is opportune to elevate your proficiency to a superior level. Please refer to the following chapter to acquire knowledge on enhancing one's persuasive abilities.

www.ingramcontent.com/pod-product-compliance
Lightning Source LLC
Chambersburg PA
CBHW050236120526
44590CB00016B/2109